CW01430530

STOP ALL THE CLOCKS
Poems of Love and Loss

W. H. AUDEN

STOP ALL THE CLOCKS
Poems of Love and Loss

faber

First published in 2025
by Faber & Faber Ltd
The Bindery, 51 Hatton Garden
London EC1N 8HN

Typeset by Faber & Faber Ltd
Printed in Poland

A CIP record for this book
is available from the British Library

ISBN 978-0-571-39682-5

2 4 6 8 10 9 7 5 3 1

CONTENTS

STOP ALL THE CLOCKS
Poems of Love and Loss

Underneath the Abject Willow

Underneath the abject willow,
    Lover, sulk no more;
Act from thought should quickly follow:
    What is thinking for?
Your unique and moping station
    Proved you cold;
    Stand up and fold
Your map of desolation.

Bells that toll across the meadows
    From the sombre spire,
Toll for those unloving shadows
    Love does not require.
All that lives may love; why longer
    Bow to loss
    With arms across?
Strike and you shall conquer.

Geese in flocks above you flying
    Their direction know;
Brooks beneath the thin ice flowing
    To their oceans go;
Coldest love will warm to action,
    Walk then, come,
    No longer numb,
Into your satisfaction.

Carry Her Over the Water

Carry her over the water,
    And set her down under the tree,
Where the culvers white all day and all night,
    And the winds from every quarter
Sing agreeably, agreeably, agreeably of love.

Put a gold ring on her finger,
    And press her close to your heart,
While the fish in the lake their snapshots take,
    And the frog, that sanguine singer,
Sing agreeably, agreeably, agreeably of love.

The streets shall all flock to your marriage,
    The houses turn round to look,
The tables and chairs say suitable prayers,
    And the horses drawing your carriage
Sing agreeably, agreeably, agreeably of love.

O Tell Me the Truth About Love

Some say that Love's a little boy
    And some say he's a bird,
Some say he makes the world go round
    And some say that's absurd:
But when I asked the man next door
    Who looked as if he knew,
His wife was very cross indeed
    And said it wouldn't do.

Does it look like a pair of pyjamas
    Or the ham in a temperance hotel,
Does its odour remind one of llamas
    Or has it a comforting smell?
Is it prickly to touch as a hedge is
    Or soft as eiderdown fluff,
Is it sharp or quite smooth at the edges?
    O tell me the truth about love.

The history books refer to it
    In cryptic little notes,
And it's a common topic on
    The Trans-Atlantic boats;
I've found the subject mentioned in
    Accounts of suicides,
And even seen it scribbled on
    The backs of railway guides.

Does it howl like a hungry Alsatian
    Or boom like a military band,
Could one give a first-class imitation
    On a saw or a Steinway Grand,
Is its singing at parties a riot,
    Does it only like Classical stuff,
Will it stop when one wants to be quiet?
    O tell me the truth about love.

I looked inside the summer-house,
    It wasn't ever there,
I've tried the Thames at Maidenhead
    And Brighton's bracing air;
I don't know what the blackbird sang
    Or what the roses said,
But it wasn't in the chicken-run
    Or underneath the bed.

Can it pull extraordinary faces,
    Is it usually sick on a swing,
Does it spend all its time at the races
    Or fiddling with pieces of string,
Has it views of its own about money,
    Does it think Patriotism enough,
Are its stories vulgar but funny?
    O tell me the truth about love.

Your feelings when you meet it, I
    Am told you can't forget,
I've sought it since I was a child
    But haven't found it yet;
I'm getting on for thirty-five,
    And still I do not know
What kind of creature it can be
    That bothers people so.

When it comes, will it come without warning
    Just as I'm picking my nose,
Will it knock on my door in the morning
    Or tread in the bus on my toes,
Will it come like a change in the weather,
    Will its greeting be courteous or bluff,
Will it alter my life altogether?
    O tell me the truth about love.

A Misunderstanding

Just as his dream foretold, he met them all:
The smiling grimy boy at the garage
Ran out before he blew his horn; the tall
Professor in the mountains with his large
Tweed pockets full of plants addressed him hours
Before he would have dared; the deaf girl too
Seemed to expect him at her green chateau;
The meal was laid, the guest room full of flowers.

More, the talk always took the wished-for turn,
Dwelt on the need for stroking and advice;
Yet, at each meeting, he was forced to learn
The same misunderstanding would arise.
Which was in need of help? Were they or he
The physician, bridegroom and incendiary?

As I Walked Out One Evening

As I walked out one evening,
    Walking down Bristol Street,
The crowds upon the pavement
    Were fields of harvest wheat.

And down by the brimming river
    I heard a lover sing
Under an arch of the railway:
    'Love has no ending.

'I'll love you, dear, I'll love you
    Till China and Africa meet,
And the river jumps over the mountain
    And the salmon sing in the street.

'I'll love you till the ocean
    Is folded and hung up to dry
And the seven stars go squawking
    Like geese about the sky.

'The years shall run like rabbits,
    For in my arms I hold
The Flower of the Ages,
    And the first love of the world.'

But all the clocks in the city
    Began to whirr and chime:

'O let not Time deceive you,
    You cannot conquer Time.

'In the burrows of the Nightmare
    Where Justice naked is,
Time watches from the shadow
    And coughs when you would kiss.

'In headaches and in worry
    Vaguely life leaks away,
And Time will have his fancy
    Tomorrow or today.

'Into many a green valley
    Drifts the appalling snow;
Time breaks the threaded dances
    And the diver's brilliant bow.

'O plunge your hands in water,
    Plunge them in up to the wrist;
Stare, stare in the basin
    And wonder what you've missed.

'The glacier knocks in the cupboard,
    The desert sighs in the bed,
And the crack in the tea-cup opens
    A lane to the land of the dead.

'Where the beggars raffle the banknotes
    And the Giant is enchanting to Jack,

And the Lily-white Boy is a Roarer,
    And Jill goes down on her back.

'O look, look in the mirror,
    O look in your distress;
Life remains a blessing
    Although you cannot bless.

'O stand, stand at the window
    As the tears scald and start;
You shall love your crooked neighbour
    With your crooked heart.'

It was late, late in the evening,
    The lovers they were gone;
The clocks had ceased their chiming
    And the deep river ran on.

Fish in the Unruffled Lakes

Fish in the unruffled lakes
The swarming colours wear,
Swans in the winter air
A white perfection have,
And the great lion walks
Through his innocent grove;
Lion, fish, and swan
Act, and are gone
Upon Time's toppling wave.

We till shadowed days are done,
We must weep and sing
Duty's conscious wrong,
The Devil in the clock,
The Goodness carefully worn
For atonement or for luck;
We must lose our loves,
On each beast and bird that moves
Turn an envious look.

Sighs for folly said and done
Twist our narrow days;
But I must bless, I must praise
That you, my swan, who have
All gifts that to the swan
Impulsive Nature gave,

The majesty and pride,
Last night should add
Your voluntary love.

Dear, Though the Night Is Gone

Dear, though the night is gone,
Its dream still haunts today,
That brought us to a room,
Cavernous, lofty as
A railway terminus,
And crowded in that gloom
Were beds, and we in one
In a far corner lay.

Our whisper woke no clocks,
We kissed and I was glad
At everything you did,
Indifferent to those
Who sat with hostile eyes
In pairs on every bed,
Arms round each other's necks,
Inert and vaguely sad.

Oh but what worm of guilt
Or what malignant doubt
Am I the victim of;
That you then, unabashed,
Did what I never wished,
Confessed another love;
And I, submissive, felt
Unwanted and went out?

Calypso

Driver, drive faster and make a good run
Down the Springfield Line under the shining sun.

Fly like the aeroplane, don't pull up short
Till you brake for Grand Central Station, New York.

For there in the middle of that waiting hall
Should be standing the one that I love best of all.

If he's not there to meet me when I get to town,
I'll stand on the pavement with tears rolling down.

For he is the one that I love to look on,
The acme of kindness and perfection.

He presses my hand and he says he loves me,
Which I find an admirable peculiarity.

The woods are bright green on both sides of the line;
The trees have their loves though they're different
    from mine.

But the poor fat old banker in the sun-parlour car
Has no one to love him except his cigar.

If I were the Head of the Church or the State,
I'd powder my nose and just tell them to wait.

For love's more important and powerful than
Ever a priest or a politician.

The Sun Shines Down on
the Ships at Sea

The sun shines down on the ships at sea,
It shines on you and it shines on me
Whatever we are or are going to be.

Tomorrow if everything goes to plan,
Tomorrow morning you'll be a man:
Let wishes be horses as fast as they can.

The dogs are barking, the crops are growing,
But nobody knows how the wind is blowing:
Gosh, to look at we're no great catch;
History seems to have struck a bad patch,

We haven't the time – it's been such a rush –
Except to attend to our own little push:
The teacher setting examinations,
The journalist writing his falsifications,

The poet reciting to Lady Diana
While the footmen whisper 'Have a banana',
The judge enforcing the obsolete law,
The banker making the loan for the war,

The expert designing the long-range gun
To exterminate everyone under the sun,
Would like to get out but could only mutter; –
'What can I do? It's my bread and butter.'

In your house tonight you are flushed and gay;
Twenty-one years have passed away;
Tomorrow morning's another day.

If we can't love, though miles apart,
If we can't trust with all our heart,
If we can't do that, then we're in the cart.

Song

Warm are the still and lucky miles,
White shores of longing stretch away,
The light of recognition fills
    The whole great day, and bright
The tiny world of lovers' arms.

Silence invades the breathing wood
Where drowsy limbs a treasure keep,
Now greenly falls the learned shade
    Across the sleeping brows
And stirs their secret to a smile.

Restored! Returned! The lost are borne
On seas of shipwreck home at last:
See! In the fire of praising burns
    The dry dumb past, and we
The life-day long shall part no more.

Lullaby

Lay your sleeping head, my love,
Human on my faithless arm;
Time and fevers burn away
Individual beauty from
Thoughtful children, and the grave
Proves the child ephemeral:
But in my arms till break of day
Let the living creature lie,
Mortal, guilty, but to me
The entirely beautiful.

Soul and body have no bounds:
To lovers as they lie upon
Her tolerant enchanted slope
In their ordinary swoon,
Grave the vision Venus sends
Of supernatural sympathy,
Universal love and hope;
While an abstract insight wakes
Among the glaciers and the rocks
The hermit's sensual ecstasy.

Certainty, fidelity
On the stroke of midnight pass
Like vibrations of a bell,
And fashionable madmen raise
Their pedantic boring cry:

Every farthing of the cost,
All the dreaded cards foretell,
Shall be paid, but from this night
Not a whisper, not a thought,
Not a kiss nor look be lost.

Beauty, midnight, vision dies:
Let the winds of dawn that blow
Softly round your dreaming head
Such a day of sweetness show
Eye and knocking heart may bless,
Find the mortal world enough;
Noons of dryness see you fed
By the involuntary powers,
Nights of insult let you pass
Watched by every human love.

The Novelist

Encased in talent like a uniform,
The rank of every poet is well known;
They can amaze us like a thunderstorm,
Or die so young, or live for years alone.

They can dash forward like hussars: but he
Must struggle out of his boyish gift and learn
How to be plain and awkward, how to be
One after whom none think it worth to turn.

For, to achieve his lightest wish, he must
Become the whole of boredom, subject to
Vulgar complaints like love, among the Just

Be just, among the Filthy filthy too,
And in his own weak person, if he can,
Must suffer dully all the wrongs of Man.

Herman Melville

(For Lincoln Kirstein)

Towards the end he sailed into an extraordinary
    mildness,
And anchored in his home and reached his wife
And rode within the harbour of her hand,
And went across each morning to an office
As though his occupation were another island.

Goodness existed: that was the new knowledge.
His terror had to blow itself quite out
To let him see it; but it was the gale had blown him
Past the Cape Horn of sensible success
Which cries: 'This rock is Eden. Shipwreck here.'

But deafened him with thunder and confused with
    lightning:
–The maniac hero hunting like a jewel
The rare ambiguous monster that had maimed his sex,
Hatred for hatred ending in a scream,
The unexplained survivor breaking off the nightmare –
All that was intricate and false; the truth was simple.

Evil is unspectacular and always human,
And shares our bed and eats at our own table,
And we are introduced to Goodness every day,
Even in drawing-rooms among a crowd of faults;
He has a name like Billy and is almost perfect
But wears a stammer like a decoration:

And every time they meet the same thing has to
    happen;
It is the Evil that is helpless like a lover
And has to pick a quarrel and succeeds,
And both are openly destroyed before our eyes.

For now he was awake and knew
No one is ever spared except in dreams;
But there was something else the nightmare had
    distorted –
Even the punishment was human and a form of love:
The howling storm had been his father's presence
And all the time he had been carried on his father's
    breast.

Who now had set him gently down and left him.
He stood upon the narrow balcony and listened:
And all the stars above him sang as in his childhood
'All, all is vanity,' but it was not the same;
For now the words descended like the calm of
    mountains –
– Nathaniel had been shy because his love was
    selfish –
But now, he cried in exultation and surrender
'The Godhead is broken like bread. We are the
    pieces.'

And sat down at his desk and wrote a story.

Our Bias

The hour-glass whispers to the lion's paw,
The clock-towers tell the gardens day and night,
How many errors Time has patience for,
How wrong they are in being always right.

Yet Time, however loud its chimes or deep,
However fast its falling torrent flows,
Has never put the lion off his leap
Nor shaken the assurance of the rose.

For they, it seems, care only for success:
While we choose words according to their sound
And judge a problem by its awkwardness;

And Time with us was always popular.
When have we not preferred some going round
To going straight to where we are?

Who's Who

A shilling life will give you all the facts:
How Father beat him, how he ran away,
What were the struggles of his youth, what acts
Made him the greatest figure of his day:
Of how he fought, fished, hunted, worked all night,
Though giddy, climbed new mountains; named a sea:
Some of the last researchers even write
Love made him weep his pints like you and me.

With all his honours on, he sighed for one
Who, say astonished critics, lived at home;
Did little jobs about the house with skill
And nothing else; could whistle; would sit still
Or potter round the garden; answered some
Of his long marvellous letters but kept none.

Ballad

O what is that sound which so thrills the ear
    Down in the valley drumming, drumming?
Only the scarlet soldiers, dear,
      The soldiers coming.

O what is that light I see flashing so clear
    Over the distance brightly, brightly?
Only the sun on their weapons, dear,
      As they step lightly.

O what are they doing with all that gear;
    What are they doing this morning, this morning?
Only the usual manœuvres, dear,
      Or perhaps a warning.

O why have they left the road down there;
    Why are they suddenly wheeling, wheeling?
Perhaps a change in the orders, dear;
      Why are you kneeling?

O haven't they stopped for the doctor's care;
    Haven't they reined their horses, their horses?
Why, they are none of them wounded, dear,
      None of these forces.

O is it the parson they want with white hair;
    Is it the parson, is it, is it?
No, they are passing his gateway, dear,
      Without a visit.

O it must be the farmer who lives so near;
     It must be the farmer so cunning, so cunning?
They have passed the farm already, dear,
          And now they are running.

O where are they going? stay with me here!
     Were the vows you swore me deceiving, deceiving?
No, I promised to love you, dear,
          But I must be leaving.

O it's broken the lock and splintered the door,
     O it's the gate where they're turning, turning;
Their feet are heavy on the floor
          And their eyes are burning.

Eyes Look into the Well

Eyes look into the well,
Tears run down from the eye;
The tower cracked and fell
From the quiet winter sky.

Under a midnight stone
Love was buried by thieves;
The robbed heart begs for a bone,
The damned rustle like leaves.

Face down in the flooded brook
With nothing more to say,
Lies One the soldiers took,
And spoiled and threw away.

Funeral Blues

Stop all the clocks, cut off the telephone,
Prevent the dog from barking with a juicy bone,
Silence the pianos and with muffled drum
Bring out the coffin, let the mourners come.

Let aeroplanes circle moaning overhead
Scribbling on the sky the message He Is Dead,
Put crêpe bows round the white necks of the public
    doves,
Let the traffic policemen wear black cotton gloves.

He was my North, my South, my East and West,
My working week and my Sunday rest,
My noon, my midnight, my talk, my song;
I thought that love would last for ever: I was wrong.

The stars are not wanted now; put out every one,
Pack up the moon and dismantle the sun,
Pour away the ocean and sweep up the wood;
For nothing now can ever come to any good.

Refugee Blues

Say this city has ten million souls,
Some are living in mansions, some are living in holes:
Yet there's no place for us, my dear, yet there's no
    place for us.

Once we had a country and we thought it fair,
Look in the atlas and you'll find it there:
We cannot go there now, my dear, we cannot go
    there now.

In the village churchyard there grows an old yew,
Every spring it blossoms anew:
Old passports can't do that, my dear, old passports
    can't do that.

The consul banged the table and said,
'If you've got no passport you're officially dead':
But we are still alive, my dear, but we are still alive.

Went to a committee; they offered me a chair;
Asked me politely to return next year:
But where shall we go today, my dear, but where
    shall we go today?

Came to a public meeting; the speaker got up and
    said;
'If we let them in, they will steal our daily bread':

He was talking of you and me, my dear, he was
     talking of you and me.

Thought I heard the thunder rumbling in the sky;
It was Hitler over Europe, saying, 'They must die':
O we were in his mind, my dear, O we were in his
     mind.

Saw a poodle in a jacket fastened with a pin,
Saw a door opened and a cat let in:
But they weren't German Jews, my dear, but they
     weren't German Jews.

Went down the harbour and stood upon the quay,
Saw the fish swimming as if they were free:
Only ten feet away, my dear, only ten feet away.

Walked through a wood, saw the birds in the trees;
They had no politicians and sang at their ease:
They weren't the human race, my dear, they weren't
     the human race.

Dreamed I saw a building with a thousand floors,
A thousand windows and a thousand doors:
Not one of them was ours, my dear, not one of
     them was ours.

Stood on a great plain in the falling snow;
Ten thousand soldiers marched to and fro:
Looking for you and me, my dear, looking for you
     and me.

Brussels in Winter

Wandering the cold streets tangled like old string,
Coming on fountains silent in the frost,
The city still escapes you; it has lost
The qualities that say 'I am a Thing'.

Only the homeless and the really humbled
Seem to be sure exactly where they are,
And in their misery are all assembled;
The winter holds them like the Opera.

Ridges of rich apartments rise tonight
Where isolated windows glow like farms:
A phrase goes packed with meaning like a van.

A look contains the history of man,
And fifty francs will earn the stranger right
To warm the heartless city in his arms.

Roman Wall Blues

Over the heather the wet wind blows,
I've lice in my tunic and a cold in my nose.

The rain comes pattering out of the sky,
I'm a Wall soldier, I don't know why.

The mist creeps over the hard grey stone,
My girl's in Tungria; I sleep alone.

Aulus goes hanging around her place,
I don't like his manners, I don't like his face.

Piso's a Christian, he worships a fish;
There'd be no kissing if he had his wish.

She gave me a ring but I diced it away;
I want my girl and I want my pay.

When I'm a veteran with only one eye
I shall do nothing but look at the sky.

A Summer Night

(*To Geoffrey Hoyland*)

Out on the lawn I lie in bed,
Vega conspicuous overhead
    In the windless nights of June;
As congregated leaves complete
Their day's activity; my feet
    Point to the rising moon.

Lucky, this point in time and space
Is chosen as my working-place;
    Where the sexy airs of summer,
The bathing hours and the bare arms,
The leisured drives through a land of farms,
    Are good to a newcomer.

Equal with colleagues in a ring
I sit on each calm evening,
    Enchanted as the flowers
The opening light draws out of hiding
With all its gradual dove-like pleading,
    Its logic and its powers:

That later we, though parted then,
May still recall these evenings when
    Fear gave his watch no look;
The lion griefs loped from the shade
And on our knees their muzzles laid,
    And Death put down his book.

Now north and south and east and west
Those I love lie down to rest;
    The moon looks on them all,
The healers and the brilliant talkers,
The eccentrics and the silent walkers,
    The dumpy and the tall.

She climbs the European sky,
Churches and power-stations lie
    Alike among earth's fixtures:
Into the galleries she peers
And blankly as an orphan stares
    Upon the marvellous pictures.

To gravity attentive, she
Can notice nothing here, though we
    Whom hunger does not move,
From gardens where we feel secure
Look up and with a sigh endure
    The tyrannies of love:

And, gentle, do not care to know,
Where Poland draws her eastern bow,
    What violence is done,
Nor ask what doubtful act allows
Our freedom in this English house,
    Our picnics in the sun.

Soon, soon, through the dykes of our content
The crumpling flood will force a rent,
    And, taller than a tree,
Hold sudden death before our eyes
Whose river dreams long hid the size
    And vigours of the sea.

But when the waters make retreat
And through the black mud first the wheat
    In shy green stalks appears,
When stranded monsters gasping lie,
And sounds of riveting terrify
    Their whorled unsubtle ears,

May these delights we dread to lose,
This privacy, need no excuse
    But to that strength belong,
As through a child's rash happy cries
The drowned parental voices rise
    In unlamenting song.

After discharges of alarm
All unpredicted let them calm
    The pulse of nervous nations.
Forgive the murderer in his glass,
Tough in their patience to surpass
    The tigress her swift motions.

The Lesson

The first time that I dreamed, we were in flight,
And fagged with running; there was civil war,
A valley full of thieves and wounded bears.

Farms blazed behind us; turning to the right,
We came at once to a tall house, its door
Wide open, waiting for its long-lost heirs.

An elderly clerk sat on the bedroom stairs
Writing; but we had tiptoed past him when
He raised his head and stuttered—'Go away.'
We wept and begged to stay:
He wiped his pince-nez, hesitated, then
Said no, he had no power to give us leave;
Our lives were not in order; we must leave.

    ★ ★ ★

The second dream began in a May wood;
We had been laughing; your blue eyes were kind,
Your excellent nakedness without disdain.

Our lips met, wishing universal good;
But on their impact sudden flame and wind
Fetched you away and turned me loose again

To make a focus for a wide wild plain,
Dead level and dead silent and bone dry,

Where nothing could have suffered, sinned, or
    grown.
On a high chair alone
I sat, a little master, asking why
The cold and solid object in my hands
Should be a human hand, one of your hands.

*   *   *

And the last dream was this: we were to go
To a great banquet and a Victory Ball
After some tournament or dangerous test.

Only our seats had velvet cushions, so
We must have won; though there were crowns
    for all,
Ours were of gold, of paper all the rest.

O fair or funny was each famous guest.
Love smiled at Courage over priceless glass,
And rockets died in hundreds to express
Our learned carelessness.
A band struck up; all over the green grass
A sea of paper crowns rose up to dance:
Ours were too heavy; we did not dance.

*   *   *

I woke. You were not there. But as I dressed
Anxiety turned to shame, feeling all three
Intended one rebuke. For had not each
In its own way tried to teach
My will to love you that it cannot be,
As I think, of such consequence to want
What anyone is given, if they want?

Musée des Beaux Arts

About suffering they were never wrong,
The Old Masters: how well they understood
Its human position; how it takes place
While someone else is eating or opening a window
    or just walking dully along;
How, when the aged are reverently, passionately
    waiting
For the miraculous birth, there always must be
Children who did not specially want it to happen,
    skating
On a pond at the edge of the wood:
They never forgot
That even the dreadful martyrdom must run its
    course
Anyhow in a corner, some untidy spot
Where the dogs go on with their doggy life and the
    torturer's horse
Scratches its innocent behind on a tree.

In Brueghel's *Icarus*, for instance: how everything
    turns away
Quite leisurely from the disaster; the ploughman
    may
Have heard the splash, the forsaken cry,
But for him it was not an important failure; the sun
    shone

As it had to on the white legs disappearing into the
    green
Water; and the expensive delicate ship that must
    have seen
Something amazing, a boy falling out of the sky,
Had somewhere to get to and sailed calmly on.

Orpheus

What does the song hope for? And the moved hands
A little way from the birds, the shy, the delightful?
     To be bewildered and happy,
       Or most of all the knowledge of life?

But the beautiful are content with the sharp notes
   of the air;
The warmth is enough. O if winter really
     Oppose, if the weak snowflake,
       What will the wish, what will the dance do?

Law Like Love

Law, say the gardeners, is the sun,
Law is the one
All gardeners obey
Tomorrow, yesterday, today.

Law is the wisdom of the old
The impotent grandfathers shrilly scold;
The grandchildren put out a treble tongue,
Law is the senses of the young.

Law, says the priest with a priestly look,
Expounding to an unpriestly people,
Law is the words in my priestly book,
Law is my pulpit and my steeple.

Law, says the judge as he looks down his nose,
Speaking clearly and most severely,
Law is as I've told you before,
Law is as you know I suppose,
Law is but let me explain it once more,
Law is The Law.

Yet law-abiding scholars write:
Law is neither wrong nor right,
Law is only crimes
Punished by places and by times,
Law is the clothes men wear

Anytime, anywhere,
Law is Good-morning and Good-night.

Others say, Law is our Fate;
Others say, Law is our State;
Others say, others say
Law is no more
Law has gone away.

And always the loud angry crowd
Very angry and very loud
Law is We,
And always the soft idiot softly Me.

If we, dear, know we know no more
Than they about the law,
If I no more than you
Know what we should and should not do
Except that all agree
Gladly or miserably
That the law is
And that all know this,
If therefore thinking it absurd
To identify Law with some other word,
Unlike so many men
I cannot say Law is again,
No more than they can we suppress
The universal wish to guess
Or slip out of our own position
Into an unconcerned condition.

Although I can at least confine
Your vanity and mine
To stating timidly
A timid similarity,
We shall boast anyway:
Like love I say.

Like love we don't know where or why
Like love we can't compel or fly
Like love we often weep
Like love we seldom keep.

On This Island

Look, stranger, at this island now
The leaping light for your delight discovers,
Stand stable here
And silent be,
That through the channels of the ear
May wander like a river
The swaying sound of the sea.

Here at the small field's ending pause
Where the chalk wall falls to the foam and its
    tall ledges
Oppose the pluck
And knock of the tide,
And the shingle scrambles after the suck-
ing surf, and the gull lodges
A moment on its sheer side.

Far off like floating seeds the ships
Diverge on urgent voluntary errands;
And the full view
Indeed may enter
And move in memory as now these clouds do,
That pass the harbour mirror
And all the summer through the water saunter.

Every Eye Must Weep Alone

(*To Chester Kallman*)

Every eye must weep alone
Till I Will be overthrown.

But I Will can be removed,
Not having sense enough
To guard against I Know,
But I Will can be removed.

Then all I's can meet and grow,
I Am become I Love,
I Have Not I Am Loved,
Then all I's can meet and grow.

Till I Will be overthrown
Every eye must weep alone.

If I Could Tell You

Time will say nothing but I told you so,
Time only knows the price we have to pay;
If I could tell you I would let you know.

If we should weep when clowns put on their show,
If we should stumble when musicians play,
Time will say nothing but I told you so.

There are no fortunes to be told, although,
Because I love you more than I can say,
If I could tell you I would let you know.

The winds must come from somewhere when they
    blow,
There must be reasons why the leaves decay;
Time will say nothing but I told you so.

Perhaps the roses really want to grow,
The vision seriously intends to stay;
If I could tell you I would let you know.

Suppose the lions all get up and go,
And all the brooks and soldiers run away;
Will Time say nothing but I told you so?
If I could tell you I would let you know.